RUPERT AND THE GREEN DRAGON

First performed at the Thorndike Theatre, Leatherhead, on 22nd January 1993, then on tour. The play was presented by Layston Productions Ltd, with the following cast:

Rupert Bear	Rachel Gaffin
Dr Chimp/The Chinese Conjurer/	
The Green Dragon	Andrew Dennis
Ottoline/Zita/Cloud Cuckoo	Pippa Lay
Pong Ping/Puppeteer/Cloud Cuckoo	A. J. Barry
Edward Trunk/Puppeteer/	
Cloud Cuckoo	David Pacquette
Bill Badger/Puppeteer (Squirrel)/	
Cloud Cuckoo	Anne Riley
Mr Bear/Puppeteer (Wise Owl)/	
Cloud Cuckoo/	
The Clerk of the Weather	Stephen Reynolds
Tigerlily/Mrs Bear/Cloud Cuckoo	Melody Brown
Podgy Pig/Cloud Cuckoo/Puppeteer	Martin Harris
Algy Pug/Cloud Cuckoo/Puppeteer	Susan Lees

Directed by David Wood
Sets and costumes designed by Susie Caulcutt
Music arranged, supervised, and incidental music written by Peter Pontzen
Musical direction and keyboards by Peter Aylin
Lighting designed by Simon Courtenay-Taylor
Magic Consultant, George Kovari

Rupert
and the Green Dragon

A musical play

Book, music and lyrics by
David Wood

Based on the *Rupert* stories and characters
by Mary Tourtel and Alfred Bestall

Samuel French — London
New York - Toronto - Hollywood

CHARACTERS
(in order of appearance)

Dr Chimp
Ottoline
Edward Trunk
Pong Ping
Algy Pug
Bill Badger
Podgy Pig
The Chinese Conjuror
Tigerlily
Rupert Bear
Squirrel (a puppet)
Wise Owl (a puppet)
Mr Bear
Mrs Bear
The Snowbird (a puppet)
The Green Dragon
Chorus of Cloud Cuckoos
The Clerk of the Weather
Zita, the Ice Maid

Financial considerations limited the number of actors used in the original production. Doubling and trebling was therefore employed. Other productions may prefer to use a larger cast.

SYNOPSIS OF SCENES

All the action can take place within one basic set, resembling a country Nutwood scene. Small trucks or flown-in pieces can change the location as necessary within this basic framework. For some of the more sophisticated puppetry scenes, it may be necessary to fly in blacks behind the action.

ACT I

SCENE 1   **Nutwood School Concert**
This introductory scene could be "in the open air". A sign or banner advertising "Nutwood School Concert" could be the only identification needed.

SCENE 2   **Nutwood Common**
This is the main basic set, which incorporates a couple of trees. These could be flown-in cut-outs or wing flats. They accommodate the puppets. One has a longish branch for Squirrel and family. The other has a hole in which Wise Owl lives.

SCENE 3   **Rupert's Home — exterior**
A cottage door with Mr Bear's hanging basket and/or window box. Mrs Bear's washing line could be a small truck set to one side.

SCENE 4   **Rupert's bedroom**
This could be on the reverse of the exterior truck. Or the exterior could fly out to reveal the bedroom. Door and bed are the only requirements.

SCENE 5   **Nutwood Common**
During this scene, snow falls, leading to the Snowbird puppetry section.

SCENE 6   **The Chinese Conjuror's House — front door and interior**
The front door could be a separate simple door in frame, which could exit as soon as Rupert and Pong Ping have entered. The interior could be a simple flown-in piece or truck, to one side of the stage, to which is added a magic cabinet and any other magic props necessary.

ACKNOWLEDGEMENTS

David Wood would like to thank Dudley Russell of Layston Productions Ltd for commissioning this play and Ian Robinson, *Rupert* Editor of the *Daily Express*, for his constructive and generous co-operation.

Cover design

SONGS

ACT I

Song 1	**Welcome to Nutwood**	Rupert, Bill, Edward, Podgy, Pong Ping, Tigerlily, Chinese Conjuror, Algy, Ottoline
Song 2	**A Sunny Day**	Edward and Rupert
Song 2A	**A Sunny Day** (reprise)	Mr Bear, Mrs Bear
Song 3	**Head in the Clouds/Cloud Cuckoo Land**	Mr Bear, Mrs Bear, Rupert
Song 4	**It's Good to Have a Special Friend**	Pong Ping
Song 5	**Follow the Snowbird**	Rupert and Pong Ping
Song 5A	**Head in the Clouds/Cloud Cuckoo Land** (reprise)	Rupert and the Cloud Cuckoos

ACT II

Song 6	**Rupert and the Green Dragon (Sky High)**	Pre-recorded Company song to accompany Puppetry section
Song 7	**Whether the Weather**	Clerk of the Weather and Rupert
Song 8	**Freeze the World**	Zita the Ice Maid
Song 8A	**It's Good to Have a Special Friend** (reprise)	Pong Ping
Song 9	**Baby Dragon Baby**	Pong Ping, Rupert, Bill, Edward, Audience
Song 9A	**Goodbye from Nutwood**	Rupert, Mr Bear, Mrs Bear, Bill, Edward, Algy, Podgy, Pong Ping, Ottoline, Green Dragon

The score, arranged by Peter Pontzen, is available on sale from Samuel French Ltd

INTRODUCTION

When I was invited to write and direct a musical play about Rupert Bear and his friends, I couldn't resist a wry smile. For the wheel had come full circle. Over twenty years ago I applied for the stage rights of *Rupert Bear*, but the *Daily Express* turned me down. At the time I was somewhat peeved because I had done quite a bit of research on the subject. I remember sitting in the Reading Room of the British Museum for days on end; either side of me eminent scholars made notes about dusty, academic tomes, while I ploughed through every published *Rupert Annual* and storybook!

I was convinced then, and remain convinced, that *Rupert* is ideal for stage adaptation. The stories combine reality and fantasy in a truly theatrical way. Mary Tourtel's original creation, later developed by the remarkable Alfred Bestall and others, has remained popular with children (and adults, I reckon) for seventy-plus years. Their appeal seems to me to consist of depicting attractive young animal characters in human clothes and situations, such as school and family life, and ferrying them from their cosy domestic existence to a fantasy world of danger, magic, fairytale, villains, kidnap, extra-terrestrial adventure, and good versus evil, with virtue triumphing before the return of the hero and his helpers to the secure and welcome normality of family tea and bedtime. In many Rupert stories there is also expressed a concern for the environment; often Mother Nature's progress is temporarily halted by some strange circumstance, and Rupert has to strive to regain the balance of the status quo.

Given the opportunity to construct a new *Rupert* story for the stage, I chose to use elements from several existing stories, but then to invent a new and potentially theatrical threat to Nutwood. Ian Robinson, the current *Rupert* Editor at the *Daily Express*, kindly allowed me to invent Zita the Ice Maid, a fugitive from the Frozen North who wants to freeze the world. Such a grand plan gives the play the "life and death" scale I believe important in a children's play. It was heartwarming when the young audiences of the first production quickly became emotionally involved in the possible fate of Rupert and his friends, cared about them enough to help them defeat Zita, and rejoiced with them when nature's balance is restored at the end.

Rupert and the Green Dragon celebrated my twenty-fifth year writing plays for children. The challenge of triggering the imaginations for first-time theatre-goers is as great as it ever was. Because, for those of us employed in children's theatre, a child's first visit to the theatre is the most important day of his or her life. We want that child to not only enjoy the experience, but to find the theatre an exciting place where stories come to life, where light, sound, music, magic, scenery, costume, actors, puppets and the spoken word combine to produce something different from, but just as valid as, a story in a book or on a large or small screen. The immediacy of the theatre experience, the communal, sometimes noisy, reaction to the twists and turns of the plot, and the willingness of young audiences to suspend their disbelief and enter whole-heartedly into the spirit of the play, make this genre of theatre unique. The actors have to be on their toes, and maintain a very high energy level. Hopefully nothing patronizing invades their performance, no looking for adult reactions over the children's heads, nothing tongue-in-cheek about their characterizations. Playing to and connecting with children demands an honesty, a simplicity, yet a highly-developed technique. I always tell my actors that working for children is the most demanding job they will ever undertake. Also the most rewarding, if we get it right!

David Wood

NOTES ON THE ORIGINAL PRODUCTION

Casting

Although it made casting quite difficult, we were determined that Rupert and his friends should all be of similar small stature; all, that is, except Tigerlily, who could be taller. Mr and Mrs Bear, Dr Chimp and the Green Dragon could be taller still. These "rules" led to the division of roles and doubling for a cast of ten. Other productions, with larger cast numbers possible, may dispense with doubling altogether, in which case it will be possible for more characters to feature in certain scenes; for instance, the song "Baby Dragon Baby" could include Tigerlily, Ottoline, Podgy and Algy — in this script they are unavailable, because the actors who portray them have other duties to prepare for! Similarly, Ottoline could attend Edward's birthday party; at present the actress playing her is in the same scene as Zita! Directors are welcome to make appropriate changes to fit their circumstances.

Set

Susie Caulcutt, who designed the original production, based her sets on the illustrations found in all the *Rupert* books and annuals; she used a basic "outdoor" set to frame all the scenes, including the "indoor" ones, most of which were mounted on trucks. Two-dimensional cut-out trees were effectively employed to house the puppet Wise Owl and the family of Squirrels. They slid on from the wings, allowing puppeteers to stand behind. They also resembled the book illustrations, helping to translate the books from page to stage.

The most complex set was the Clerk of the Weather's weather station, which took up most of the stage and had several moving gadgets, flashing lights and Heath Robinson-esque machinery. We used specially designed slides to illustrate the weather song, but illustrations on boards or a flip chart would have been satisfactory.

The whole set, however, was designed for basic simplicity, to enable the scene changes to take place speedily, usually in view of the audience. Long delays when changing the scene lead to children losing concentration; far better to let them *see* what is going on, maybe in silhouette, as shapes truck or fly in and out.

Props

Most of the props were straightforward, although some invention was necessary to make the flowers grow from the window box (a lever operated from inside the house made them rise magically), and making Bill Badger's baby brother pop his head up over the side of his pram became a task for a skilled prop-maker! A toy badger in the pram would have worked nearly as well; Bill could have taken him out and held him.

Puppetry

The Wise Owl and the Squirrels were glove puppets. Wise Owl had a beak and eyes that opened and closed. He, like all the puppets, was specially made.

The Snowbird was a large, exotic puppet, operated on rods by two puppeteers, who wore blacks to make them merge into the black curtains behind. The rods gave considerable height to the Snowbird's flight, successfully giving the impression that she was leading Rupert and Pong Ping through the snow.

The *optional* UV Puppetry sequence at the beginning of Act II consisted of quite large puppets — Rupert sitting on the Green Dragon — held and operated by puppeteers in blacks against black tabs. The other flying objects were cut-outs on rods.

Magic

George Kovari, the Magic Adviser on the original production, provided the necessary props and expertise to make the magic effective. Directors of other productions are strongly advised to consult a member of the local Magic Society, or contact the Magic Circle for someone to advise. I cannot undermine the rules of the Magic Circle by revealing the secrets of the tricks in this Acting Edition, but I can give some signposts which will lead any experienced magician to at least one way of achieving the necessary effects. In the opening concert, our Chinese Conjurer first performed a showy, "silent", oriental trick such as producing flowers in a special "rabbit pan" production bowl or, using a similar prop, turning flames into flowers. Then he showed both sides of his cloak and produced from it his daughter, Tigerlily. Finally they used a "doll's house" illusion cabinet to produce Rupert; this was decorated in oriental pagoda style.

When Tigerlily magically made drinks for Rupert and Pong Ping she used a variation of the classic "Water to Wine" trick, coupled with the use of a "lotus vase", which can be shown empty several times while still retaining several "loads" of liquid.

The Dragon Cabinet which achieves the magical substitution of Rupert and Pong Ping, resembled a pagoda. Two cloaks were necessary, one hidden from the outset in the floor of the cabinet. *Two* spring blinds covered the front; one had a large picture of a dragon, the other had a black shape in place of the dragon. The stage directions in this Acting Edition should be enough for a magic adviser to work out the routine.

We decided *not* to magically melt and disappear Zita, mainly because we felt that it was too drastic a "final solution", even for a "baddie" character! And, in any case, an illusion to achieve this effectively might be too bulky!

Costumes

Susie Caulcutt based her designs as closely as possible on the familiar illustrations in the *Rupert* books and annuals. Zita, the only new character, was dressed in a flowing, diaphanous gown and tiara headdress, conveying the idea of cool, elegant beauty; icicles hung from her sleeves and she carried an icicle wand.

The Cloud Cuckoos wore clown-like puffball costumes to give the idea of both clouds *and* cuckoos.

All the animals needed some kind of headdress to resemble the familiar characters. But we decided not to completely cover up the actors' faces. Animal "helmets" were devised which fitted tight to the back of the head, but in front only came to eyebrow level. Thus the animal's face sat above the actor's face. The audience could sometimes see *both* faces, but theatrical licence made it perfectly acceptable. In mimed sequences, the actors lowered their own heads, making them invisible to the audience; at these times the illusion of the animals was total.

Our headdresses were made by a skilled craftsman — at considerable cost. Other productions may use simpler ones. But it is, I feel, important that the characters, so well known from books and television, are recognizable!

Music

Peter Pontzen's arrangements and incidental music based on my songs are included in the Vocal Score, available from Samuel French Ltd. Music is often used as underscoring, as in a film, and for linking between scenes. We used two keyboard synthesizers, which gave richness and variety to the score.

Lighting

We decided to avoid Black-outs whenever possible and let the action flow smoothly from scene to scene. Scenery flying out and trucks arriving and departing were often done in full view. The puppets needed special attention to ensure they were clearly visible.

Sound

Taped sound effects proved useful. Birdsong on Nutwood Common; the voices of the baby squirrels; the baby badger's cries; thunder and wind for the Snowbird sequence; various whooshes for the Green Dragon's take-off; the pre-recorded song at the start of Act II; the clock chimes; mechanical cog and dial noises in the Weather Station; the sound of machinery jamming; the coming of Spring. Other effects and noises were provided by the keyboard synthesizers.

David Wood

To Rupert and Zita Syme,
with special thanks to Zita for letting me use her name —
for a baddie character too!

David Wood

ACT I

SCENE 1

The Nutwood School Concert

As the House Lights go down, the ringing of a school handbell is heard

Through the front of house tabs comes Dr Chimp, ringing the bell, clutching notes

Dr Chimp Ladies and gentlemen. Young ladies, young gentlemen. Hallo! (*The audience is encouraged to respond*) Welcome to Nutwood School, where I, Doctor Chimp, am the long-serving, long-suffering teacher. Today is a special day, the last day of the Spring term, and to celebrate, the pupils of Nutwood School perform for you their end of-term Springtime Concert.

He rings his bell as a fanfare, then refers to his notes

And first, let's have a big cheer for my newest pupil:
The most talented otter you've ever seen —
Queen of the keyboard, it's Ottoline!

He rings his bell and gets caught up in the curtains as they rise or part, revealing a banner announcing "Nutwood School Concert". A piano is to one side

As the audience cheer, encouraged by Dr Chimp, Ottoline enters shyly. She does a nervous curtsy, then sits at the piano. Dr Chimp exits

Surprisingly, she suddenly starts to play a difficult piece of classical music, technically flamboyant and impressive. After a few bars, the style changes to a more rum-te-tum foot-tapping style, as a vamp over her introductions

Ottoline (*in rhythm, to the audience*) All join in my guessing game
I'll give you clues, you shout the name!
First here comes our big strong friend
With a trunk at the front and a tail at the end!

Who is it? Yes, it's Edward Trunk! Give him a cheer!

Edward Trunk enters and bows. Music continues as he briefly exits, then returns, pulling strongly over his shoulder a thick rope. He disappears off the other side as the rope continues travelling across

Eventually he appears from the first side (having dashed across unseen behind the scenery) hanging on to the end of the rope, which pulls him off the other side

Alternatively, Edward Trunk enters, bows and prepares, like a weight lifter, to lift a heavy-looking set of dumbbells pre-set downstage

With much wobbling and "strong" acting, he manages to lift the dumbbells above his head, then lower them to the floor

Chord as he takes his applause and exits

Ottoline notices he has left the dumbbells on the stage

(*Whispering*) Edward!

No reaction. Ottoline, with a shrug, leaves the piano, goes to the dumbbells, and, with ease, picks them up in one hand and takes them off with an embarrassed smile. She returns and sits at the piano, re-starting her rhythmic vamp

>A pekinese from Old Peking
>Please clap your hands and meet ...
>Who is it? Yes! ... Pong Ping!

Pong Ping enters and spins an oriental plate or two. He takes a bow, then exits

>Now another Nutwood pal, gee
>Here's a pug by the name of ...
>(*Encouraging the audience to shout out*) Algy!

Algy Pug enters, carrying a cardboard box. His act is deliberately corny, encouraging groans

Algy Hallo! Would you like to see me fly? (*He produces a giant rubber joke fly*) Buzz buzz! Here's me fly!

Boos from off

Would you like to see me tap dance? (*He produces a tap on a string*) Here's me tap, see him dance! (*He makes the tap dance*)

Boos from off

NB: The following section is optional

Would you like to see my water otter? (*He produces a kettle*) Here it is! My water otter!

Boos from off stage (and by now, hopefully, the audience)

End of optional section

Algy exits

Ottoline   Now here's an act with style and skill
                      Please welcome a badger by the name of ...
                      (*Encouraging the audience to shout out*) Bill!

Bill Badger enters. He does a brief juggling act using three apples

Bill   Here's a friend who's big but not stodgy
                      Say hallo to a pig called ...
                      (*Encouraging the audience to shout out*) Podgy!

Podgy Pig enters

Podgy Bill, I've got a puzzle for you.
Bill Ready, Podgy.
Podgy How many apples have you got?
Bill Three.
Podgy Right. If you give me *one* apple, (*he takes one*) how many have you got left?
Bill Er ... two.
Podgy Right. If you give me *another* apple, (*he takes another*) how many have you got left?

Bill Er ... one.
Podgy Right. If you give me *another* apple, (*he takes another*) how many
    have you got left?
Bill Er ... none!
Podgy Right. And how many apples have *I* got?
Bill Er ... three.
Podgy Right! Lucky old me! Yum, yum, yum!

He runs off eating, chased by Bill

Ottoline Now, you've met nearly everyone. But someone's still to come.
    Who is it?
Audience Rupert!
Ottoline Who?
Audience Rupert!
Ottoline Yes!

> Wave your hands up in the air
> And say hallo to Rupert Bear!

But he doesn't enter

Pong Ping, Algy, Podgy and Bill creep on and whisper to Ottoline

Oh, sorry. He's not here yet. So er ... instead, please welcome Tigerlily,
with her father, the Chinese Conjuror!

All stand watching by the piano as:

*Tigerlily and her father enter. (NB: In the original production, the Chinese
Conjuror entered alone and magically "produced" Tigerlily from his
cloak.) They perform an oriental magic trick, then bring on a small "Doll's
House". It is shown empty*

Chinese Conjuror Now see Rupert appear by magic! (*Waving his wand*)
    Abracadabra!

*Tigerlily opens the door of the Doll's House. A soft-toy Rupert is discovered.
The Chinese Conjuror and Tigerlily react dismayed. The door of the "Doll's
House" is shut again, leaving the miniature Rupert inside*

Tigerlily (*to the audience*) Please help us! Everybody say Abracadabra!

Audience (*conducted by Tigerlily*) Abracadabra!

A flash. From the "Doll's House" up pops Rupert Bear. He wears a school satchel

Cheers and applause

Rupert Hallo everybody! And welcome! Welcome to ...

Song 1: Welcome to Nutwood

(*Speaking*) N.U.T.
(*Singing*) Double U Double O D
Nutwood! Nutwood!
That's the place to be
Nutwood is the place for me!

The others join him (except Ottoline, who plays the piano)

Ottoline	And me!
Algy	And me!
Podgy	And me!
Tigerlily	And me!
Chinese Conjuror	And me!
Bill	And me!
Edward	And me!
Pong Ping	And me!

All   N.U.T.
Double U Double O D
Nutwood! Nutwood!
That's the place to be;
Nutwood is the place for me!

So light the lights,
Off we go,
Play the music,
It's the start of the show.

We've learnt our words
Rehearsed each song,
Fingers crossed
We won't go wrong.

Rupert   It's good to see you
                        Glad you came
                        We hope you will
                        Feel the same

All   In
                        N.U.T.
                        Double U Double O D
                        Nutwood! Nutwood!
                        That's the place to be
                        Nutwood is the place for me!

                        Nutwood! Nutwood!
                        Nutwood green and fair
                        Nutwood is the place for —

The following lines are spoken

Ottoline   Ottoline!
Algy   Algy Pug!
Podgy   Podgy Pig!
Tigerlily   Tigerlily!
Chinese Conjuror The Chinese Conjuror!
Bill   Bill Badger!
Edward   Edward Trunk!
Pong Ping   Pong Ping!
Rupert   And Rupert Bear!
All (*singing*)   And Rupert Bear!
                        Rupert Bear!

Rupert steps forward, while the others gather upstage

The Chinese Conjuror exits

Rupert Thank you. Now, everybody, my friends and I would like to tell you
a story. It's called ...

Fanfare

"Rupert and the Green Dragon". It all started one Friday afternoon. After
school, we were all setting off home when ——
Edward Hey, Rupert, don't go without this!

Rupert turns and enters the scene. Edward is handing out envelopes

   Algy, Ottoline, Podgy, Tigerlily, Bill, Pong Ping ...

All thank Edward

   ... and Rupert.
Rupert Thanks, Edward. What is it?
Edward An invitation. To my party tomorrow. (*Shyly*) You see, it's my
   birthday.

All cheer

   (*Rather morose*) Hope you can all come. There'll be a special tea and party
   games.
All Great, thanks Edward, see you tomorrow, bye, *etc.*

   *All except Edward and Rupert leave. They take the piano and the
   "Nutwood School Concert" banner with them*

Edward seems rather sad

Rupert (*sensing Edward's gloom*) See you at the party then, Edward. And
   happy birthday!
Edward Yes. Thank you, Rupert.
Rupert You don't seem very excited about it.
Edward (*sighing*) I am. I am. Parties are very exciting things.
Rupert What's the matter then?
Edward It's just whether the weather ...
Rupert Whether the weather?
Edward Whether the weather will be warm enough.
Rupert It *is* a bit chilly for Springtime.
Edward My mum says it's too cold to have the party on Nutwood Common.
   You see, Rupert, our house is too small for a proper party.
Rupert Maybe the weather will brighten up tomorrow.
Edward (*sighing*) Maybe. (*Nodding gloomily*) It's best to look on the bright
   side.
Rupert Listen, Edward, what would you like for a birthday present? A
   bouncy ball? A book to read?
Edward How kind you are, Rupert. Quite frankly, the best present you could
   give me would be ...
Rupert What?

Song 2: A Sunny Day

Edward (*speaking*)   All I want is
                         A sunny day,
        (*Singing*)   A sunny day
                         Would make me smile.
                         All I want is
                         A sunny day,
                         We haven't had
                         A sunny day
                         For a long long while.

                         All I want is
Rupert   A sunny day,
Edward   A sunny day
                         Is what I'd choose.
                         All I want is
Both   A sunny day,
                         A sunny day
                         On Nutwood Common
                         Would be good news.

                         A sunny day
                         Would raise our spirits
                         And give us all a lift.
Edward   A sunny day
                         For me
                         I'd say
                         Would be
                         The perfect birthday gift.

Both   All I want is
                         A sunny day,
                         A sunny day
                         Would make me smile.
                         All I want is
                         A sunny day,
                         We haven't had
                         A sunny day
                         For a long long while.

> A sunny day,
> A sunny day,
> A sunny day,
> A sunny day!

As the song ends, Edward waves and leaves

Music continues as Rupert stands, thoughtful

Rupert Poor old Edward. I wish I could help. Better go home. That means crossing Nutwood Common.

Background birdsong could continue through the Nutwood Common scene

SCENE 2

Nutwood Common

Rupert sets off. Suddenly a voice stops him

Squirrel (*off*) A-a-a-tishoo!

Rupert looks for where the sound is coming from

A-a-a-tishoo! A-a-a-tishoo!

Squirrel emerges from behind a tree and sits on a branch. Hopefully the audience sees her and directs Rupert to her

Rupert Hallo, Squirrel. How are you?
Squirrel Fed up.
Rupert Fed up?
Squirrel Me nose is froze, me teeth are chatter-chattering, my paws are freezing and I keep sneezing. Atishoo!
Rupert (*handing her a hanky*) Use my hanky.
Squirrel A hanky! Thankee!

She blows loudly into the hanky held by Rupert

Rupert Blow! And again!
Squirrel Thank you, Rupert. Sorry I'm so down in the dumps. But it's so cold.
Rupert I know. Edward's fed up too. It's his birthday tomorrow.

Squirrel That's nice. What are you giving him?
Rupert Well, all he wants is a sunny day.
Squirrel Huh! Don't we all! Atishoo!

High-pitched chattering noises from the tree

Quiet! (*To Rupert*) It's my babies, bless 'em. They want to leave the nest, but it's far too chilly. They're hungry, too. And I'm out of nuts.
Rupert I've got a peanut butter sandwich they can have.

He produces it from his satchel and gives it to Squirrel

Squirrel Bless you, Rupert, you're a very kind bear.
Rupert Giving your babies a sandwich is easy. I wish it was easy to give Edward his sunny day.
Squirrel Listen, go and see Wise Owl. He knows everything about everything. Ask his advice.
Rupert Thanks, Squirrel, I will.
Squirrel Bye, Rupert. Atishoo!

Chattering from her babies

I'm coming! I'm coming! Atishoo!

She disappears

Music as Rupert continues his journey. He does a circuit of the stage before arriving at Wise Owl's tree

Rupert (*calling*) Wise Owl!

No reply

Wise Owl!

Rupert goes to look behind the tree as Wise Owl emerges from his hole

Possible audience participation as they see him before Rupert — when Rupert comes round again, Wise Owl has returned inside, etc. Eventually Rupert sees him

There you are. Hallo, Wise Owl.

Wise Owl You've woken me up, little bear. (*He yawns*)

Rupert Sorry, but I have a problem.

Wise Owl It's far too cold for problems.

Rupert But that *is* the problem.

Wise Owl It is indeed. Come back when it's warmer. (*He yawns and starts to retreat into his hole*)

Rupert No, please! Wise Owl, my friend Edward wants a sunny day for his birthday. How can I give him one?

Wise Owl A sunny day. (*He yawns*) That would be nice. (*He appears to go to sleep*)

Rupert Don't go to sleep, please!

Wise Owl (*irritable*) I'm not asleep. You woke me up. I'm thinking. I close my eyes to help me concentrate.

Rupert Well?

Wise Owl (*oracle-like, almost as though in a trance*) Go to see the Clerk of the Weather.

Rupert The Clerk of the Weather?

Wise Owl He is in charge of the wind and the rain and the sun and the snow. (*He yawns*) He might help, you never know!

Rupert Where does he live?

Wise Owl Questions, questions. He lives at his Weather station up in the sky beyond the clouds (*He yawns*) Goodbye, little bear, it's too chilly to chatter. Good luck.

He retreats inside his hole

Rupert But how do I get there? How ... he's gone. (*Calling*) Thank you, Wise Owl.

Music as Rupert thoughtfully leaves the tree. He does a circuit of the stage as the scene changes to:

Scene 3

Rupert's Home — exterior

A window-box and/or hanging-basket (empty) is by the door. There is a washing line

Mr Bear is sweeping the "path"

Rupert approaches

Rupert Hi, Dad!
Mr Bear Hallo, son. Good day at school?
Rupert Fine, Dad. Good day in the garden?
Mr Bear 'Fraid not, son.
Rupert Why, what's happened?
Mr Bear Nothing's happened. Nothing at all. Look at my seedlings.

Rupert looks in the window box

Rupert Can't see anything, Dad.
Mr Bear Exactly, son. There's nothing to see. They haven't grown. It's
   meant to be Springtime, Rupert. By now the flowers should be opening.
   But there's no sign of stalks, let alone flowers.
Rupert Maybe they need watering, Dad.

He finds a watering can and tries pouring

   Hey, Dad!
Mr Bear Mm?
Rupert The water. It's gone solid! It's ice!
Mr Bear I tell you, son, the weather's gone topsy-turvy. Ice in Spring. It's
   not natural.
Rupert It's a real mystery.

Mrs Bear comes out of the door with a washing basket

Mrs Bear Hallo, Rupert.
Rupert Hi, Mum.
Mrs Bear Good day at school, dear?
Rupert Fine, Mum. Good day at home?
Mrs Bear Well, I got all the washing done. Tea's on the table and then it's
   bedtime.
Rupert Thanks, Mum.

Rupert goes inside

Mrs Bear goes to the washing line and removes a shirt

Mrs Bear Oh no. Look! (*She holds up a very stiff shirt*) It's frozen stiff. What
   is the weather up to?

Mr Bear swings other frozen clothes on the line

Song 2A: A Sunny Day (reprise)

Mr Bear ⎱   All we want is
Mrs Bear ⎰   A sunny day,
                   A sunny day
                   Would suit us fine.
                   All we want is
                   A sunny day,
Mrs Bear   A sunny day
                   Would dry the clothes
                   On my washing line.

Both   All we want is
                   A sunny day,
                   A sunny day
                   Would please us so.
                   All we want is
                   A sunny day,
Mr Bear   A sunny day
                   Would make the seeds
                   In my garden grow.

Both   A sunny day,
                   A sunny day,
                   A sunny day,
                   A sunny day.

Music continues

The Lights crossfade as the scene changes to:

SCENE 4

Rupert's bedroom

Rupert is in bed reading a book

Mr and Mrs Bear enter

Mrs Bear Good-night, Rupert.

Rupert Night, Mum. Night, Dad.

Mr Bear Night, son. Anything exciting happening tomorrow?

Rupert I've been invited to Edward Trunk's birthday party. Can I go, Mum?

Mrs Bear Of course you can. It'll be fun.

Mr Bear What are you giving him for a present?

Rupert A sunny day.

Mr Bear A sunny day?

Rupert That's what he'd like.

Mrs Bear That's what we'd all like, Rupert. But how can you give him a sunny day?

Rupert I'm going to see the Clerk of the Weather, Mum. Up in the sky beyond the clouds. He'll fix it, I'm sure.

Mr Bear Oh, son ...

Mrs Bear You and your fanciful schemes and dreams.

Mr Bear How will you get there?

Rupert Somehow, Dad, somehow.

Mrs Bear Oh, Rupert ....

Song 3: Head in the Clouds/Cloud Cuckoo Land

Mrs Bear ⎞
Mr Bear ⎠
(*singing*) You've got your
Head in the clouds,
Your feet off the ground,
Your nose in the air.
You've got your
Head in the clouds,
You seem
To live in a dream.

Mrs Bear (*speaking*) You're living in Cloud Cuckoo Land!

Rupert Where's that, Mum?

Mrs Bear Cloud Cuckoo Land? There's no such place! Except in your head!

Mrs Bear ⎞
Mr Bear ⎠
(*singing*) Cloud Cuckoo Land is for Cuckoos,
Cuckoos who don't know what's what,
Cloud Cuckoo Land
May seem grand
To you,
But we can assure you it's not.

Cloud Cuckoo Land is for dreamers,
Dreamers who get nothing done.

> Cloud Cuckoo Land,
> Understand,
> Is not
> The land for the likes of our son.

Music continues

Rupert (*speaking*) I'd like to go to Cloud Cuckoo Land.
Mr Bear I'm sure you would, son, but you're better off with both feet firmly on the ground.
Mrs Bear Like your dad and me.
Rupert But if we don't have dreams, dreams can never come true. And mine is only a little dream. All I want is a sunny day for Edward. (*He sings*)

The following verses are sung in counterpoint

> All I want is
> A sunny day,
> A sunny day
> For Edward's
> Birthday,
> All I want is
> A sunny day;
> A sunny day for
> Edward's birthday
> Is my dream,
> Is my dream

Mr Bear   You've got your
Mrs Bear   Head in the clouds,
> Your feet off the ground,
> Your nose in the air.

> You've got your
> Head in the clouds,
> You seem

> To live in a dream,
> In a dream.

Music continues

Mrs Bear (*whispering*) Good-night, Rupert.

Mr Bear (*whispering*) Good-night, son.

Rupert is asleep

Mr and Mrs Bear leave, turning off the light

SCENE 5

Nutwood Common

Music as the lighting slowly fades up to represent dawn rising. A visual interlude treat! Birdsong

Pong Ping enters. He carries a kite. Music continues as he tries to fly it. He throws it up in the air, but it drops. He throws it higher but it falls on his head. He places it to one side, then pulls the string, but it simply drags along the ground towards him. He gets cross and stamps his foot

Pong Ping There's an old Chinese proverb that says "Many hands make kite work". I need more hands! (*He sings*)

Song 4: It's Good to Have a Special Friend

It's good to have
A friend to fly
A kite with,
To learn to write
Or stay the night
Or have a fight with,
A friend who never lets you down,
On whom you can depend,
It's good to have a special friend.

It's good to have
A friend to go
To school with,
To swim a pool
Or break a rule
Or play the fool with,
A friend you can be honest with
But know you won't offend,
It's good to have a special friend.

Bouncing a ball
Against a wall
Will do,
But it's better
If you get a
Special friend
To throw it to.

It's good to have
A special friend
To be with ...

He breaks off as he notices somebody coming

Music continues as Ottoline enters carrying a music case

(*Speaking*) It's Ottoline. Hi, Ottoline!
Ottoline Morning, Pong Ping.
Pong Ping Would you like to fly my kite with me?
Ottoline I'd love to, Pong Ping, but I've got a piano lesson this morning.
Sorry. Bye.

She goes

Pong Ping Bye.

He looks downcast, then perks up as Bill Badger enters pushing a pram

It's Bill Badger. Hi Bill!
Bill Morning, Pong Ping.
Pong Ping Would you like to fly my kite with me?
Bill I would.
Pong Ping Good!
Bill But I can't. I've got to look after my baby brother this morning. I'm
taking him for a walk.
Pong Ping Oh. (*Looking in the pram*) Morning Baby Badger!

*The Baby Badger pops his head out of the pram (or Bill takes him out), opens
his mouth and screams blue murder*

Bill You've woken him up!

Pong Ping Sorry.

The baby screams

Bill It's all right, baby. (*He makes soothing noises*) Pong Ping won't hurt you. He's my friend.

The baby screams. Pong Ping reacts

Do you want to come with us, Pong Ping?
Pong Ping Er ... no, thank you. Bye.
Bill Bye.

Bill Badger exits with the pram

Pong Ping continues singing

Pong Ping   It's good to have
                      A special friend
                      To be with,
                      To climb a tree
                      Or eat your tea
                      Or disagree with,
                      A friend who thinks the same as you
                      Who makes a perfect blend,
                      It's good to have a special friend.

                      Maybe you like
                      To ride a bike
                      — I do! —
                      But it's kinda
                      Nice to find a
                      Special friend
                      To ride with you.

                      It's good to have
                      A friend who you
                      Feel sure with ...

He breaks off as he notices somebody coming

Music continues as Podgy Pig enters, eating from a bag of buns

(*Speaking*) It's Podgy Pig! Hi Podgy!

Podgy (*with his mouth full*) Morning, Pong Ping. Fancy a bun?
Pong Ping Yes, please.
Podgy Sorry, there's none left.
Pong Ping Oh. Listen, Podgy, would you like to fly my kite with me?
Podgy Sorry, I'm off to Nutwood Station to meet my cousin Rosalie.
Pong Ping What's she coming for?
Podgy She's coming for ... breakfast. And elevenses. And lunch. And tea.
And supper. And dinner. And cocoa ...

He has gone

Pong Ping Bye, Podgy.

Edward Trunk enters carrying boxes of food and other things for his party.
Party hats on the top. Maybe Edward wears one. The load is so tall that
Edward can't see where he is going

Who's this? Hallo! Who's there?
Edward (*still walking*) Me.
Pong Ping Who's me?
Edward *I'm* me.
Pong Ping (*going round to see*) It's Edward Trunk. Hi Edward!
Edward Morning, Pong Ping.
Pong Ping What are you doing?
Edward Taking all these things home for my party.

He nearly falls off the stage. Pong Ping stops him

Pong Ping You're going the wrong way, Edward.
Edward What?
Pong Ping Your home is in *that* direction.

He turns him round

Edward Thanks, Pong Ping. Lucky I met you. It's good to have friends.

He goes, unsteadily

Pong Ping Yes, it is. (*Calling*) You wouldn't like to ... (*He holds up his kite*)
No, of course you wouldn't.

Suddenly Algy Pug enters on a bicycle (or Pogo stick)

Algy Look out, Pong Ping! Wheeee!
Pong Ping (*jumping out of the way*) Hi Algy! Would you like ...
Algy Can't stop. Just got the hang of it. Wheeee!

He zooms off the same way as Edward exited

Pong Ping Careful, Algy! Edward Trunk's just ——

A crash from off. Pong Ping covers his eyes

Pong Ping continues singing

> It's good to have
> A friend who you
> Feel sure with,
> To go explore
> Or paint and draw
> Or share a straw with.
> A friend who's always on your side
> Until the bitter end,
> It's good to have a special friend.
>
> It's good to have
> A friend to lick
> Ice cream with,
> To fish a stream,
> Support a team
> Or share a dream with,
> A friend who makes you laugh, who some-
> Times drives you round the bend ...
> A friend who never lets you down
> On whom you can depend,
> A friend you can be honest with
> But know you won't offend
> A friend who thinks the same as you
> Who makes a perfect blend
> A friend who's always on your side
> Until the bitter end.
> It would be good to have a special friend.

Rupert enters

Rupert Good-morning, Pong Ping.

Pong Ping (*grumpy*) Morning, Rupert. Not much good about it.

Rupert It's cold, yes.

Pong Ping It's not that.

Rupert What's the matter, then?

Pong Ping Oh nothing.

Rupert You can tell me. I'm your friend.

Pong Ping Oh yes, everyone's my friend till I ask them to play with me. I suppose you're busy too.

Rupert Well I am, actually. I'm off to see the Clerk of the Weather.

Pong Ping The Clerk of the Weather? Who's he?

Rupert He's in charge of the weather. I'm going to ask him for a sunny day for Edward's birthday present.

Pong Ping (*brightening*) Could I come with you?

Rupert Of course. If I only knew how to get there.

Pong Ping Where?

Rupert To his weather station. Up in the sky beyond the clouds.

Pong Ping Up in the sky! Wow!

Rupert Exactly.

Pong Ping (*suddenly*) Rupert Fly my kite!

Rupert Well, thanks Pong Ping, but I really ought to be off.

Pong Ping Yes, yes! Off on the end of my kite! Up into the sky.

Rupert Well ...

Pong Ping (*giving Rupert the kite*) Come on, you hold the string ...

Music as they try to fly the kite. Pong Ping throws it in the air, Rupert tugs the string. But all to no avail

Rupert (*eventually*) It's no good, Pong Ping. There's no wind. The only way this kite could fly is by magic.

Pong Ping Magic! The Chinese Conjuror and Tigerlily! Let's go and ask them!

Rupert Good idea, Pong Ping! Come on!

They set off, to music, but suddenly a crack of thunder stops them. The sky darkens

Quick!

They start to walk. Snow starts to fall. Music as they struggle along

They possibly exit

The snow becomes more blizzard-like as blacks fly in behind

> *Rupert and Pong Ping reappear, clinging on to each other, and trying to press forward*

Pong Ping (*eventually*) Where are we, Rupert?
Rupert I don't know. I think we're lost.
Pong Ping Oh Rupert, what are we going to do?

> *Suddenly, lit up against the blacks, the Snowbird enters. Perhaps it utters a birdcry*

Rupert Look! It's the Snowbird! (*Calling*) Snowbird, we're lost! Please can you help us find the Chinese Conjuror's house?

Perhaps the Snowbird calls a birdcry meaning "follow"

Come on, Pong Ping! She's leading the way.

During the song, in an attractive puppetry sequence, the Snowbird leads Rupert and Pong Ping round the stage as the snow continues to fall

Song 5: Follow the Snowbird

(*Singing*)

Follow the Snowbird,
Follow;
She shines through the darkness,
She lights up the skies.
Come on,
Follow the Snowbird,
Follow;
Trust her and follow
Wherever she flies.

Rupert ⎫
Pong Ping ⎭

Follow the Snowbird,
Follow;
We're lost and in danger
But somehow she knows,
So we

Follow the Snowbird,
Follow;
Trust her and follow
Wherever she goes.

A blizzard is blowing,
There's no way of knowing
Where we have come
Or where we are going.
Our worry is growing,
Till suddenly glowing,
The Snowbird appears
Melting our fears.

Follow the Snowbird,
Follow;
She'll guide us to safety,
We won't go astray
If we
Follow the Snowbird,
Follow,
Trust her and follow,
She'll show us the way.

Trust her and follow,
Trust her and follow,
Trust her and follow,
(the Snowbird, follow)
Through the snow.

As the song ends, a door becomes visible. Rupert rings a bell

Rupert Thank you, Snowbird!

The Snowbird calls farewell and exits

SCENE 6

The Chinese Conjuror's House

Tigerlily opens the door

Tigerlily Rupert! Pong Ping!

Rupert Can we come in, Tigerlily?
Tigerlily Of course.

Rupert and Pong Ping enter

*Lights fade up on a section of the Chinese Conjuror's living-room. There is
an oriental sideboard*

It's so cold. It should be Springtime.
Pong Ping It should.
Rupert That's really why we're here. You see ...
Tigerlily Wait. Chinese hospitality says I must welcome you with a drink.
Rupert Thank you.

*From the sideboard Tigerlily brings two glasses and hands them to Rupert
and Pong Ping. Then she collects an opaque "Lotus vase"*

Music as Tigerlily "performs" the magic drink-pouring

Tigerlily Rupert. What is your favourite drink?
Rupert Lemonade, please.

Tigerlily pours lemonade into Rupert's glass. The vase is now empty

Thank you.
Pong Ping Oh, it's all gone.
Rupert You can have some of mine ...
Tigerlily Wait! Pong Ping. What is your favourite drink?
Pong Ping Cherryade, please.

*Tigerlily makes a magic pass, then pours a cherryade (red) from the vase into
Pong Ping's glass. The vase is now empty*

Thank you. But what about you?
Rupert There's none left!
Tigerlily I like limeade!

*She makes a magic pass, collects another glass, then pours a limeade (green)
from the vase into the glass. She bows. The others clap*

Chinese cheers!

All drink, then replace their glasses and the vase on the sideboard

Now tell me, why have you come? We're seeing each other at Edward's party aren't we?

Rupert Well, yes, but Edward wants a sunny day for his birthday present, and Wise Owl told me to ask the Clerk of the Weather ...

Pong Ping ... who lives up in the sky, beyond the clouds ...

Rupert ... yes, but I can't get there ...

Pong Ping ... except by magic ...

Rupert ... yes, so Pong Ping suggested your father might help. Do you think he would?

Tigerlily I'm sure he would!

Rupert Good.

Pong Ping Good.

Tigerlily But he can't. He's away, doing a magic show.

Rupert Oh.

Pong Ping No!

Disappointed pause

Tigerlily (*suddenly*) I tell you what!

Rupert What?

Tigerlily Maybe *I* could try some magic.

Pong Ping Yes!

Rupert Well ...

Tigerlily It would be fun, Rupert.

Rupert Not if it went wrong.

Tigerlily I've seen my father do it. It looks easy enough.

Pong Ping Can I have a go too?

Tigerlily You can be my assistant.

Rupert But, Tigerlily ...

Tigerlily Put this on.

She gives Pong Ping an oriental robe

I'll fetch my father's spare magic wand.

Rupert Yes, but ...

Tigerlily exits

I hope she knows what she's doing.

Pong Ping Hey, Rupert, (*displaying the robe*) how do I look? Ladies and Gentlemen, for my next trick ...

He picks up a tin and opens it. A huge snake pops out

Aaaaah!

Rupert (*laughing*) Serves you right, Pong Ping! You shouldn't play with magic.

Pong Ping, realizing the snake is harmless, puts it out of sight

Tigerlily returns, wearing an oriental robe and carrying a magic wand

Tigerlily Right. Stand by, everybody.

She positions Rupert

Rupert Do be careful, Tigerlily.
Tigerlily Don't worry, Rupert. It's easy!
Rupert Good luck!

Tigerlily adopts a magic stance, holding up the wand, chanting

Tigerlily   Rupert wants to reach the sky,
                      Abracadabra, make him fly!

She waves the wand. Flash. Pause, then Rupert suddenly bursts into tears, crying and sobbing

Pong Ping What's going on?
Tigerlily Oh no! I haven't made him fly, I've made him cry!
Pong Ping That's no good!

More crying and sobbing from Rupert

Tigerlily I'll have to say the magic word backwards, to reverse the magic.

She takes up her magic stance

Arbadacarba!

She waves the wand. Flash. Rupert stops crying

Rupert What happened?

Tigerlily Sorry, Rupert. The magic ——
Pong Ping Didn't work.
Tigerlily Well, it *worked*, but ... let's try something else!
Rupert Well, I don't know, Tigerlily, maybe ...
Tigerlily The magic dragon cabinet!
Rupert What's that?
Tigerlily It makes things disappear.
Pong Ping Great!
Rupert I don't want to disappear!
Tigerlily It'll be fun, Rupert, you'll see. Come with me, Pong Ping.
Rupert But ...

Too late. Tigerlily and Pong Ping have gone off

Music as Rupert waits, somewhat concerned

Tigerlily and Pong Ping, both dressed in oriental cloaks, return with an oriental magic cabinet

The back and sides have various patterns painted on, but the front has a spring blind decorated with a green dragon. Rupert stands to one side as Tigerlily releases the spring blind. The cabinet is empty. Tigerlily invites Rupert to step inside. Warily he does so. Tigerlily pulls down the spring blind. Then Tigerlily and Pong Ping circle the cabinet with exaggerated movements. Both re-emerge downstage. The music intensifies as Tigerlily steps forward and holds up her wand

Tigerlily   Abracadabra, hey presto
                         Rupert, ready, steady, go!

(*She goes back to the cabinet*) Rupert, have you gone?
Rupert (*from inside the cabinet*) No, Tigerlily, I'm still here!
Tigerlily Oh.

She walks round the cabinet, as before, with exaggerated movements; Pong Ping follows. Tigerlily re-emerges downstage

(*Seeing the audience*) Maybe ... please would you all help? Say the magic words after me?
Audience Yes.
Tigerlily Thank you. Abracadabra.
Audience Abracadabra.

Tigerlily Hey presto.
Audience Hey presto.
Tigerlily Rupert, ready, steady, go!
Audience Rupert, ready, steady, go!

A flash. Tigerlily goes to the cabinet and releases the blind. Pong Ping is revealed inside

Tigerlily Pong Ping! What are you doing in there?
Pong Ping (*coming out dazed*) I don't know, I ...
Tigerlily (*going to her "Assistant"*) But, I don't understand ... *this* was you!

She pulls off the "Assistant's" robe, revealing Rupert

  Rupert! But how ...? I'm sorry. Magic's not as easy as I thought.
Rupert Don't worry, Tigerlily, you did your best.

Tigerlily pulls down the spring blind

Tigerlily I really thought the dragon cabinet would do the trick.

She doesn't notice that the dragon on the spring blind has disappeared, leaving a cut-out hole, or a blacked-out shape. Maybe the audience notices and shouts out

Rupert Maybe I'll never reach the Clerk of the Weather. Maybe Edward
  won't get his sunny day after all. It can't be helped.

Pong Ping (hopefully led by the audience) has spotted that the dragon has disappeared

Pong Ping Hey, look everyone! The green dragon!
Tigerlily (*depressed*) What about it?
Pong Ping It's gone!
Tigerlily It can't have gone. It ... (*She looks and sees*) It's gone!
Pong Ping Told you. It's magic.
Rupert But it can't have disappeared.
Tigerlily It has. What will my father say? Quick, let's put the cabinet back.

  They all push it off

Rather sinister music as a real Green Dragon enters the other side. It stalks around, then looks off and, seeing the others return, exits or hides

The others enter. The audience will probably try to tell them about the Dragon

Pong Ping That was a great trick. The disappearing dragon.
Tigerlily But Rupert was meant to disappear, not the dragon. My father will be ——

Music as the Dragon appears. He starts to advance threateningly towards Rupert and co. Hopefully the audience shout out a warning. In any event, they suddenly turn to see him

All Aaaaaah!

The Dragon chases them off

All four reappear and chase across the stage and off

And again

Then the Dragon alone enters, stops, and mimes sobbing. He stands c looking forlorn

The heads of Rupert, Pong Ping and Tigerlily peep round the side

Rupert He's stopped. He's taking deep breaths.
Pong Ping Maybe he's doing his exercises.
Tigerlily You don't think he's trying to breathe fire, do you? Dragons can. They have very hot breath.
Rupert He's not a very big dragon.
Pong Ping He may be a baby dragon. And those deep breaths — I think they're sobs. He's crying.

Pong Ping advances towards the Dragon. The others gingerly follow

Rupert Careful, Pong Ping.
Pong Ping Hallo, baby Dragon!

The Dragon reacts. All react. The Dragon sobs more

He *is* crying. It's all right. We don't want to hurt you. And you don't want to hurt us, do you?

The Dragon shakes his head

There, there! (*To the others*) See, he's friendly.

The Dragon hugs him, lifting him off the ground

Rupert He's very strong!
Pong Ping (*laughing*) Put me down, Dragon!

The Dragon puts him down

Now, I'm Pong Ping.

The Dragon bows

This is Tigerlily.
Tigerlily Hallo, Green Dragon.

The Dragon bows

Rupert And I'm Rupert.

The Dragon bows

We're your friends!

The Dragon hugs him and lifts him up, or tickles him

Pong Ping He's saying he's *our* friend too.

The Dragon puts Rupert down and does a little dragon dance of pleasure

Rupert (*an idea*) Tigerlily, I've just thought. Why is the Green Dragon here?
Tigerlily Because my magic went wrong, that's why.
Rupert But what if it *didn't* go wrong?
Tigerlily Of course it went wrong, Rupert. I was trying to fly you to the Clerk of the Weather and you're still here!
Rupert But the Green Dragon's here too. Your magic brought him here. And surely dragons can ——
Tigerlily Fly! Of course.
Rupert (*going to the Dragon*) Green Dragon, will you help me?

The Dragon nods

My friend Edward wants a sunny day for his birthday and I'm going to ask
the Clerk of the Weather for one. Can you fly me there? Up in the sky
beyond the clouds?

The Dragon nods and indicates to Rupert to climb aboard. He does so

Tigerlily Good luck, Rupert.
Pong Ping Safe journey!
Rupert Thank you. Ready, Green Dragon?

The Dragon nods

> Dragon please carry me up in the sky
> Stand by for countdown, Nutwood goodbye!

The Dragon "revs up"

All (*encouraging the audience to join in*) Ten, nine, eight, seven, six, five,
four, three, two, one, lift off!

*Sound effects and magical lighting changes to suggest take-off. Lots of
smoke! It may be best to black out first, or use a strobe effect*

Rupert We're flying! We're flying!

*Pong Ping and Tigerlily exit, waving goodbye to Rupert and the Green
Dragon*

SCENE 7

Cloud Cuckoo Land

*When a brighter lighting state returns, Rupert and the Dragon appear to be
above the clouds (possibly dry ice) against a blue background. Maybe there
are other cut-out clouds at each side*

Music as Rupert looks excitedly around

Song 5A: Head in the Clouds/Cloud Cuckoo Land (reprise)

Rupert   I've got my
                      Head in the clouds,
                      My feet off the ground,
                      My nose in the air.
                      I've got my
                      Head in the clouds,
                      I seem
                      To be in a dream.

Suddenly, from behind the clouds, all around Rupert and the Dragon, appear the Cloud Cuckoos, who then accompany the song

   (*Speaking*) Who are you?
Cuckoos Whoo? Ooo! Cuckoo! Cuckoo! Cuckoo!
Rupert Cuckoos! Then I must be in Cloud Cuckoo Land!
Cuckoos Cuckoo! Cuckoo! Cuckoo! (*They sing*)

                      Cuckoo! Cuckoo!
                      Cuckoo! Cuckoo!
                      Cuckoo! Cuckoo!
                      Cuckoo! Cuckoo!

Rupert So soon I'll reach the Clerk of the Weather! Edward may get a sunny
   day after all! (*He sings*)

The following verses are sung in counterpoint

                      Cloud Cuckoo Land is
                          for dreamers,
                      Dreamers with plenty to do;
                      Cloud Cuckoo Land
                      Is the land
                      For me
                      Where maybe my dream
                          will come true.
                      Cloud Cuckoo Land
                      Is the land
                      For me
                      Where maybe my dream
                          will come true.

Cuckoos   Cuckoo! Cuckoo!
                      Cuckoo! Cuckoo!

Cuckoo! Cuckoo!
Cuckoo! Cuckoo!

Ah
Cuckoo!
Cuckoo! Cuckoo!

Cuckoo!
Ah
Cuckoo!
Ah

Cuckoo!

A final tableau as Rupert and the Cuckoos wave

Black-out

CURTAIN

ACT II

SCENE 1

The Sky

NB: this scene is optional and may be omitted if the puppetry is impractical; if so, it is suggested that the song is still used to introduce the next scene

A UV/puppetry sequence — perhaps black theatre — in which Rupert, sitting aboard the Dragon, flies through the sky on his journey. They encounter other flying objects, such as birds, aeroplanes, flying saucers, a hot air balloon, etc. A mirror-ball could give the effect of a starry sky. The appearance could be magical or cartoon-like

During the sequence a pre-recorded song accompanies the action

Song 6: Rupert and the Green Dragon (Sky High)

Voices
Rupert and the Green Dragon,
Racing through space,
Beyond the clouds in search of
A very special place.
A voyage of discovery,
The Dragon in full flight,
And on his back sits Rupert Bear:
Good luck and hold on tight!

See them fly,
Fly, fly.
See them fly
Sky high.

Rupert and the Green Dragon
Zoom on their way,
Determined to achieve
Operation "Sunny Day".
The Dragon swoops and loops the loop

Till Rupert feels quite ill;
He wishes he'd had time to take
An anti-sickness pill!

See them fly,
Fly, fly,
See them fly
Sky high.

Rupert and the Green Dragon
Speed on their quest.
It's cold and Rupert's glad that
He wore a woolly vest.
A day trip through the Universe,
No time to take a nap;
A myst'ry tour to who knows where
They've flown clear off the map!

See them fly,
Fly, fly.
See them fly,
Sky high
Sky high
Sky high.

SCENE 2

The Clerk of the Weather's Weather Station in the Clouds

A Heath Robinson-inspired office with levers, dials, charts, and moving cogs and wheels. A main console with flashing lights and a very large visual display screen. The main lever can point to sections ranging from "Big Freeze" to "Heatwave". At the start of the scene it points to "Big Freeze". Nothing is working normally and the only lights that flash are red. The screen is out of action

The Clerk of the Weather is slumped at his console

There is a knock at the door. Rupert enters gingerly, followed by the Dragon

Rupert Hallo! Clerk of the Weather! Can we come in? (*Looking around*) Gosh, Dragon, look!

They eventually come to the slumped Clerk. The Dragon spots him first and taps Rupert, making him jump

Aaaah! What is it?

The Dragon points to the Clerk. They both approach him. A loud snore from the Clerk makes them both jump

He's asleep.

The Dragon mimes "Wake him up"

Wake him up? Do you think we should?

The Dragon nods and mimes flying

We've flown a long way to see him? True. (*Softly*) Excuse me. Clerk of the Weather!

Another big snore makes Rupert jump. The Dragon shakes the Clerk quite roughly

Careful!

The Clerk wakes up

Clerk (*as if in a nightmare*) No! No! Please! No! (*He suddenly sees Rupert*) Aaaaah!
Rupert It's all right, Clerk of the Weather. It's me. Rupert Bear. From Nutwood.
Clerk How do you do.
Rupert And this is my friend, the Green Dragon.

The Clerk turns and sees the Dragon

Clerk Aaaah!
Rupert He's only a baby dragon. And he's very friendly.

The Dragon bows politely

Clerk How do you do. (*To Rupert*) Where am I?

Rupert In your weather station. You are the Clerk of the Weather, aren't you?

Clerk Am I? Yes, yes. Of course I am. (*He shudders*) Forgive me. Welcome. I'm rather confused. And I'm so cold.

Rupert *You're* cold? So is Nutwood. That's why we're here. You see ──

Clerk Wait! Cold, cold! I remember. No, I don't. (*He thinks*) Somebody came here. Somebody ... (*He can't remember*) No, it's gone. (*Suddenly*) What day is it?

Rupert Saturday.

Clerk Saturday ...

He looks at his calendar. It says Wednesday

But my calendar says Wednesday. I've lost three days. For three days I must have been slumped where you found me. Out cold. (*He shudders*) Very cold. Oh, Rupert, something very strange has been going on.

Rupert It has. It's a real mystery. In Nutwood it's so cold it's started snowing.

Clerk Snowing? But that's highly irregular. It should be Springtime in Nutwood. Warm sun. Flowers growing.

Rupert Yes.

Clerk Snowing? It's unbelievable. It's unnatural. It's ... (*He suddenly starts checking dials. He reaches the main lever*) It's a disaster! Look, Rupert. The master lever. It's pointing to Big Freeze. You know what this means?

Rupert It means Nutwood is going to freeze?

Clerk Not just Nutwood. *Everywhere!* The whole world is going to freeze.

Rupert But that's terrible ... can't we stop it?

Clerk We can try. We *must* stop it. I'll pull the lever back. (*He tries to pull the lever. It won't budge. He strains harder. He examines the lever*)

Rupert Is it stuck?

Clerk Worse. It's frozen solid. Iced up. This could be the start of another Ice Age. The end of life as we know it.

Suddenly the Dragon, who has stayed thoughtful, bounces into life, miming that he wants to help

Your Dragon's in a bit of a flap. Don't blame him. *I'm* in a bit of a flap.

Rupert I think he's trying to tell us something. (*To the Dragon*) What?

The Dragon mimes help

You want to help?

The Dragon nods

But how? How could you help?

The Dragon starts miming breathing

(*To the audience*) What's he saying?

Hopefully the audience say "Hot breath" or "Breathing fire"

Of course! (*To the audience*) Thank you! (*To the Clerk*) He might be able
to unfreeze the master lever, with his hot breath.
Clerk It's worth a try. I can't budge it.
Rupert Come on, Green Dragon. Do your stuff!

*Music as the Dragon goes to the lever. He summons up a deep breath. And
another. Rupert and the Clerk stand clear, then check the lever. Another
breath*

Clerk I think it's working! More! More!

More breaths

It's melting!

One more breath

I think he's done it ...

He tries the lever. It moves

Yes ...

*It moves to "warm". Immediately lights on the console flash green and other
dials and cogs start working*

The master lever is working again!

Rupert cheers

Thank you!

Rupert Well done, Green Dragon!
Clerk I think it's no exaggeration to state that thanks to Rupert and the Green
  Dragon, the world has been saved! Please (*searching on the console*)
  accept this as a small token of my gratitude.

He gives Rupert a miniature barometer

Rupert Thank you, Clerk of the Weather. What is it?
Clerk It's a personal barometer for telling the weather. Keep it in your
  bedroom to tell you what the weather will be like each morning.
Rupert I will. (*He pockets it*)
Clerk Now you two have helped me. What can I do for *you*?
Rupert (*thinking*) Of course! This is why we came, really. I very much want
  to give my friend Edward a sunny day for his birthday.
Clerk Ah. Certainly. When is it?
Rupert Today. His party's this afternoon.
Clerk I see. Well, thanks to you, (*pointing to the lever*) Nutwood will be
  warming up already. But ... let me see ... er, yes ... (*He punches information
  into the console*) Nutwood. Sun. Three o'clock. How's that?
Rupert Thank you. That's perfect.
Clerk Now, allow me to show you round. Tell you a bit about how the
  weather works.
Rupert Yes, please.
Clerk (*showing his console*) This is where it all happens. (*Indicating the big
  screen*) And this is my sort of window on the weather. You see, Rupert ...

*During the song, the Clerk of the Weather activates the big screen, which
shows slides, video or computer graphics to illustrate the song*

Song 7: Whether the Weather

(*Speaking*)We'd find it very boring
(*Singing*) If the days were all the same,
      So to balance all the elements
      Of weather is my aim.
      Not too hot
      And not too cold,
      Not too wet
      And not too dry;
      To always get it right
      Is impossible — but I try.

The earth is wrapped in a cloak of air
"The Atmosphere" we call it, and the weather's made up
    there.
The air moves round, and believe it or not,
When it's cold it falls, but rises when it's hot.
This air may be just a gentle breeze:
It ruffles up your hair and it rustles through the trees.
Sometimes it's a wind to fly a kite or fill a sail,
But sometimes it brings danger, blowing up a mighty gale.

Whether the weather
Be sunshine or storm,
Whether the weather
Be chilly or warm,
We know that whatever
The weather may bring,
Without it we'd never
See summer or spring,
Or autumn or winter,
Or year follow year.
Without weather
We wouldn't be here.

A vapour forms when Earth's water dries;
It's carried by the warm air up, up, up into the skies
The vapour turns back to water again.
Which collects in clouds and falls to earth as rain.
The bigger the cloud the more it pours
And ev'ryone gets wet if they venture out of doors.
If it's freezing cold inside the cloud, you're sure to know,
'Cos then the vapour turns into a shower of hail or snow.

Clerk ⎫
Rupert ⎬   Whether the weather
Be sunshine or storm,
Whether the weather
Be chilly or warm.
We know that whatever
The weather may bring,
Without it we'd never
See summer or spring,
Or autumn or winter,
Or year follow year.

                     Without weather
                     We wouldn't be here.

Clerk   The sun shines down ev'ry single day;
                     We cannot always see it 'cos the clouds get in the way.
                     It cheers us up with its comforting glow
                     And it warms the Earth so trees and plants can grow.
                     The weather has lots to learn about,
                     Like thunder, lightning, floods, typhoons, hurricanes and
                         drought.
                     Fogs and frosts and fronts and heatwaves, isobars and ice
                     Be sure you never ever get the same old weather twice.

Both   Whether the weather
                     Be sunshine or storm,
                     Whether the weather
                     Be chilly or warm,
                     We know that whatever
                     The weather may bring,
                     Without it we'd never
                     See summer or spring,
                     Or autumn or winter,
                     Or year follow year.
                     Without weather
                     We wouldn't be here.

Clerk (*speaking*) So, Rupert, next time the weather in Nutwood changes,
    think of me!
Rupert I will. Thank you.

*Suddenly the big screen goes fuzzy. Then the sound of machinery jamming
interrupts the scene. All the flashing lights on the console go out, except the
red ones*

Clerk What on earth ...?

*The face of Zita, the Ice Maid, appears on the screen, smiling evilly. Tension
music. Perhaps a cackle of laughter*

Rupert Who's that?
Clerk It's ... (*remembering*) Zita!
Rupert Zita?

Clerk The Ice Maid from the Frozen North. She's cold as ice, she's hard as ice, she's *made* of ice. I remember now. She came here. She's the one who ... oh Rupert, this is serious! She froze the master lever!

Rupert But why?

Clerk She wants to freeze the world. She's evil, Rupert. She wants to change the balance of nature. She must have realized we'd got things working again.

Rupert (*pointing to the console*) But everything's *stopped* working again.

Clerk Indeed it has. Oh dear, oh dear. (*He tries a few knobs and switches*) Nothing! Nothing! (*Looking in an instruction manual*) What's to do? What's to do? (*Slamming it shut*) Quick! The main generator in the engine room downstairs! Maybe I can ... oh dear, oh dear. You and your Dragon come too, Rupert. Quick! Emergency! Emergency!

They all exit at speed, off the side opposite the door

Suddenly the picture on the screen disappears as, accompanied by a flash, Zita enters the Weather Station

Zita   Tremble, quiver, quake with fear
                            Now you've had it! Zita's here!

(*She cackles*) How's it going, Clarkie? The world freezing nicely? The world getting ready to welcome its new Queen?

                            A world where all is snow and ice
                            And I'm in charge! How very nice!

(*She gives another cackle. She looks to where she had left the Clerk of the Weather*) Well, Clarkie? (*She turns and sees he has gone*) Aha! Not here! (*She sees the master lever*) And the lever free! Aha! I thought as much. I smell trickery. I smell deceit. I smell ... (*seeing the audience*) Earthlings. Clarkie has little visitors. Well, well, well. Perhaps they know what's been going on. (*Addressing the audience sweetly*) Do you?

Audience No.

Zita Would you nice, sweet little earthlings kindly tell Zita where the dear Clerk of the Weather is?

Audience No.

Zita I see. (*An idea*) Zita might have a nice ice lolly for you if you tell. You'd like that, wouldn't you?

Audience No.

Zita I warn you, little earthlings, Zita may get cross.

Zita always gets her way
Zita always wins the day!

Song 8: Freeze The World

(*Singing*) From the icy wastes of the frozen north
Zita made her escape and ventured forth.
Why should I stay for years and years
Where I've nothing to do, where I'm bored to tears?
Now I'm free,
Wait and see.

I'll freeze the World
I'll seize the World
I'll freeze the seas
The fields, the trees
To minus a thousand degrees;
Make the World a giant ball of ice,
My perfect paradise!

Little Earthlings you may not like me much,
But be warned, if you feel my icy touch,
You will be frozen in a trice,
So you'd better be nice, that is my advice!
Just take care,
Just beware!

I'll freeze the World
I'll seize the World
I'll freeze the seas
The fields, the trees
To minus a thousand degrees;
Till the World is white instead of green,
And Zita will be Queen!

(*Speaking*) You have one final chance. Will you help me?
Audience No.
Zita Very well. You've asked for it!

Watch what Zita's going to do
(*She takes hold of the lever*)
Freeze the world and freeze you too!

Tension music, as she starts to move the lever

Rupert suddenly enters

Hopefully the audience shout a warning, which stops Zita in her tracks. Rupert sees her

Rupert Don't do it, Zita! Don't.
Zita Who are you?
Rupert Rupert Bear from Nutwood.
Zita You interfering brat of a bear. How dare you meddle with me!
Rupert You can't freeze the world!
Zita I can and I will!
Rupert It's wrong to change the balance of nature. (*Advancing*) You mustn't!
Zita I warn you, Rupert Bear. Don't come near me. One touch and you're frozen.

Rupert carries on bravely as Zita starts to move the lever

Rupert Stop!

He goes to grab the lever, but Zita grabs him. There is a high-pitched musical screech as Rupert succumbs to her icy touch. He struggles, but eventually submits and slumps, frozen, on the lever. Zita cackles

Zita   Stupid bear to cross with Zita
                       No-one in the world can beat 'er!

Now for the Big Freeze. (*She tries to reach the lever. She strains to reach it*) Aaaah. I can't move the lever. The wretched Rupert is frozen to it! Aaaaa! (*She comes forward, furious*) Revenge, revenge! How can Zita punish this interfering trickster? Aha! Nutwood. He said he was from Nutwood. If I can't freeze the world, I'll freeze Nutwood! (*She cackles*)

                       Look out, Nutwood, Zita comes,
                       To freeze all Rupert's little chums!

(*To the audience*) And that includes you!

She cackles and exits through the door

The Clerk of the Weather and the Dragon return from the other side

Clerk Rupert, where are you?

He and the Dragon look anxiously for Rupert. The audience guide them to him

Rupert! Thank heavens! I thought ... (*He realizes Rupert isn't responding*) Rupert! Oh dear, oh dear! What's happened?

The Dragon gets the Clerk of the Weather's attention

What?

The Dragon points to the audience

Of course!

They come forward

(*To the audience*) What's happened to Rupert? (*Interpreting the audience's information*) He's been frozen? ... Who froze him? ... Zita? ... You mean Zita was here? ... And she tried to push the lever and ... Rupert tried to stop her? ... What's to do? What's to do?

As the Clerk of the Weather flaps about, the Dragon encourages the audience to tell the Clerk that he will try to unfreeze Rupert

What? What's he saying? Oh yes, of course! Green Dragon, do your stuff!

Music as the Dragon summons up a deep breath. And another. The Clerk of the Weather checks Rupert

It's no good! He's still frozen solid.

The Dragon indicates the audience

What? Everyone could help?

The Dragon mimes deep breathing

Everyone could breathe hot air? Yes! (*To the audience*) Come on everyone! Breathe hot breath! To save Rupert!

The Dragon leads

Ready? Breathe! Breathe! Breathe!

Rupert starts to unfreeze. The Clerk of the Weather checks Rupert

It's working! And again! Breathe! Breathe! Breathe! Breathe!

Rupert regains full control

We did it! Hooray! (*He encourages a cheer from the audience*)
Rupert (*hugging Dragon*) Thank you, Green Dragon.

The Dragon indicates the audience

Thank you, too!
Clerk Rupert, you were very brave. Single-handed you've beaten Zita!
Rupert Zita! Where is she? (*He looks about. To the audience*) Where's she
gone?
Audience Nutwood!
Rupert Nutwood?
Audience Yes!
Rupert Why?

The audience tells him

To freeze it? Oh no!
Clerk Rupert, it's up to you. You must save Nutwood!
Rupert I'll try. Come on, Green Dragon! (*He climbs aboard*) Goodbye,
Clerk of the Weather. And thank you.
Clerk Goodbye, Rupert. And good luck!

Rupert   Dragon, please, as fast as you can
                         Carry me back to where we began!

They encourage the audience to joint the countdown

Rupert } (*together*) Ten, nine, eight, seven, six, five, four, three, two,
Clerk }   one, lift-off!

Black-out as Rupert and the Dragon start to fly off. A whooshing sound effect

SCENE 3

Nutwood Common

Music

As the scene change takes place, the Lights come up on the downstage area

Pong Ping, Bill Badger, Tigerlily, Algy Pug and Podgy Pig enter excitedly, all carrying birthday presents for Edward Trunk. They put the parcels down and unfold a long banner. They stretch it between them. It reveals a message, but it's upside down. Hopefully the audience point out to them it is upside down. In any event, they eventually realize, and turn it over. They proudly display it once more. This time it is back to front, so the wording is invisible to the audience. Again the audience hopefully realize it is wrong and tell them, "Turn it round". They try again, reversing the positions of the line-up. This time it correctly reads: "HAPPY BIRTHDAY TO EDWARD TRUNK". By this time the scene change should have finished. We are back at Nutwood Common. The lighting should not be too bright, suggesting a fine day rather than a sunny one

Edward's friends erect the banner at the back of the stage as the music builds to Edward's entrance. All cheer him as he comes on and encourage the audience to join in, and, by pointing to each word on the banner, shout out the message. Meanwhile Edward opens one or two presents, including a toy trumpet

All (*including the audience*) Happy birthday to Edward Trunk!

All cheer, and then they all sing "Happy Birthday" to Edward

> *During the last line of "Happy Birthday", Bill dashes off and brings on a birthday cake with lighted candles*

Calls for Edward to "blow". He does. The candles go out. Cheers

Edward Thank you everybody. And welcome to my party!

Cheers

> Now, who would like to play a party game?

All except Podgy Pig put their hands up

All (except Podgy) Yes! Me! (*etc.*)
Podgy I'd rather eat some birthday cake.
Edward Later, Podgy, later. Let's play ... musical statues.
All Yes!
Edward Now I'll play my new toy trumpet and you all dance around, bounce
   up and down or hop about. But when I stop playing the music you all have
   to stop and stay still as a statue. The first person to wobble is out. All right?
All Yes!
Edward Here we go then.

*He starts playing his trumpet. All leap around. He stops playing. All stop and
stand still except Bill Badger*

   Bill! You're out!
Bill (*realizing*) Oh no! That's not fair. I didn't hear the music stop! Please!
Edward All right. We'll say that was a trial run. Now it's for real. Ready?

*He plays the trumpet. Everyone leaps around. He stops playing. Everyone,
including Edward, stands still, in odd positions. Silence*

   Suddenly Rupert enters, unseen by the others

Rupert (*horrified*) Oh no! I'm too late. Zita must have got here before us and
   frozen everybody! (*Unable to believe his eyes, he wanders among them*)
Edward (*suddenly*) Rupert! You're out!
Rupert What?
Edward You moved!

Everyone comes to life, laughing

Rupert But I thought ——
Edward We're playing musical statues!
Rupert I see. It's your party! Sorry I'm late, Edward. Happy birthday.
Edward Thank you, Rupert. And thank you for my present. A fine day.
Rupert Well, you *wanted* a sunny day, Edward.
Edward A fine day is ... fine !

   *The Dragon enters. Pong Ping and Tigerlily react pleased, but the others
   scream and scatter*

Pong Ping (*going to the Dragon*) It's all right. It's the Green Dragon. He's only a baby Dragon. And he's very friendly. Aren't you?

The Dragon bows politely to everyone

Rupert And he's very helpful.
Edward He can come to my party if he likes.

The Dragon nods happily

Tigerlily How did you get on, Rupert?
Pong Ping Did you see the Clerk of the Weather?
Rupert Yes. And ... (*Suddenly realizing*) Zita!
Pong Ping Zita?
Rupert The Ice Maid. She's cold as ice, she's hard as ice. She's made of ice. She's ——

Zita cackles loudly, off, interrupting them

She's here! Quick, everyone, hide!

All scatter. Perhaps some go into the audience and hide there

Zita enters. She looks around

Zita   Tremble, quiver, quake with fear
                           Now you've had it, Zita's here!

(*Another cackle. Suddenly, to the audience*) Is this Nutwood?
Audience (*hopefully*) No!
Zita I think it is! (*Seeing the birthday presents*) Mm. Signs of a birthday party. Well, soon it will be Zita's turn to celebrate. Nutwood looks a nice place to live. Even nicer when it's icy and hard and cold and beautiful. Like me! Now, to business. Rupert's dear little friends. I'll sniff 'em out and stiffen 'em solid. One touch of my freezing fingers and they'll be in my clutches! (*She cackles*)

                           There's no escape you little fools
                           Zita's cool and Zita rules!

She cackles and exits

Rupert and friends return to the stage

Tigerlily She's gone.
Rupert She'll be back. And she'll try to freeze us. (*He includes the audience*)
All of us!
Edward What are we going to do?
Bill Quick, Rupert, think of something.
Rupert I'm thinking, I'm thinking.

Suddenly the Dragon steps forward, tapping Rupert on the shoulder

What is it, Green Dragon?

The Dragon points to his head

You've got an idea?

The Dragon nods, then freezes

Freeze? I know, Zita's going to freeze us.

The Dragon shakes his head

No?

The Dragon indicates everybody, including the audience

All? All freeze?
Edward (*understanding*) Like musical statues!
Rupert Of course! We could all freeze and fool Zita into thinking we're
already frozen!
Tigerlily Then she won't *need* to freeze us.
Rupert Then what?

The Dragon mimes hot breathing

Breathing? Hot breathing?

The Dragon indicates the audience too

All do hot breathing?

The Dragon nods, then mimes melting

And make Zita melt? Melt and disappear forever? Well, it's worth a try. (*To the audience*) Will you all help us?
Audience Yes!
Rupert You will?
Audience Yes!
Rupert Thank you. We'd better have a practice. Tigerlily, you pretend to be Zita.
Tigerlily Right. Er ... (*Practising*)

> Tremble, quiver, quake with fear
> Now you've had it, Zita's here!

The others applaud

Rupert (*thinking it through*) Brilliant! And then we all start the hot breathing. We need a signal.
Edward Use my trumpet, Rupert.
Rupert (*receiving it*) Good idea. Now everybody. Freeze. Arms in the air! Still as a statue. Like in the game. Don't move a muscle! Freeze!

All freeze, including the audience. When all is still ...

(*Whispering*) Go, Tigerlily.
Tigerlily (*improvising*) Er ...

> This won't please you
> Zita's going to freeze you!

Oh! Look! They're frozen already!
Rupert (*blowing the trumpet*) Breathe! Breathe!

All blow hot breaths towards Tigerlily, who mimes melting

Tigerlily Ah! Ahhh! Help!

She jumps up as the practice finishes

Rupert That's brilliant! Well done, everyone!

Zita cackles loudly, off, interrupting them

Pong Ping She's coming! She's coming!
Rupert Right. This time it's for real! Don't forget, everyone. Wait for the
signal ... (*he does a quick blast on the trumpet*) then let Zita have it! Now,
arms in the air! Still as a statue! Freeze! Now, I'd better hide. Zita thinks
I'm still frozen at the weather station.

He hides, having checked everyone, including the audience, is still

Zita enters. She suddenly sees Rupert's friends

Zita (*to the audience*) Aha! Rupert's wretched little friends ready for the
deep freeze. (*Suddenly she realizes everyone is still. Wandering amongst
them*) But look! The little dears are frozen already! (*She cackles*) When I
froze Rupert, I must have moved the master lever after all. My plan is
working! They're all frozen! (*Looking at the audience*) Even the little
earthlings! Nutwood is mine! The world is mine! (*She cackles*)

Rupert suddenly enters

Rupert (*blowing the trumpet*) Now! Breathe! Breathe!

*All, including the audience, come to life and breathe hot breaths at Zita, with
the Dragon to the fore. Rupert's friends surround Zita, who is thus trapped.
A dramatic lighting effect*

Zita (*as the hot breaths continue*) No! No! It's hot! It's so hot!
Rupert Breathe! Breathe!
Zita (*seeing him*) Rupert Bear! But how? I froze you! Aah! Zita is
sweltering! Zita is melting! Mercy! Mercy!
Rupert Only if you promise to return to the Frozen North and never to try
and change the balance of nature again. No more freezing!
Zita I promise! I promise!

She exits at speed

*NB: alternatively, using a magic illusion, Zita could really melt and
disappear. But maybe that would be too final ...*

*All cheer, sharing their pleasure with the audience. A clock begins to chime.
Rupert calms everyone to listen. Three chimes*

Rupert Three o'clock! Time for your present, Edward.

Music accompanies a transformation scene. The lighting brightens as the sun dramatically appears in the sky. Flowers grow — perhaps they are large cut-out flowers which pivot in from the wings and/or "grow" upstage. Birdsong. All look around in wonder

(*Stepping forward*) The danger's past. Spring is here at last! (*Looking up*) Thank you, Clerk of the Weather!

All cheer

Edward Thank you, Rupert! For my sunny day. And for saving Nutwood!

All cheer

Rupert (*to the audience*) Thank you, everyone who helped. Especially our new friend, the Green Dragon!

All cheer

Well, I suppose it's time to go home.

Music as all turn to leave their separate ways, Edward collects his presents

Perhaps Algy and Podgy take off the birthday banner

Tigerlily exits, but the others are still visible

The Dragon is left behind, looking lonely

Bill (*suddenly*) What about the Green Dragon?
Edward He has no home to go to.
Pong Ping (*after a pause*) He can come and live with me. If he'd like to. (*He sings*)

Song 8A: It's Good To Have A Special Friend (reprise)

It's good to have
A special friend
To play with,
To spend the day,
To fly away
Or go and stay with

He stretches out his arms. The Dragon goes to Pong Ping. They hug

> A friend who never lets you down,
> On whom you can depend,
> It's good so good to have a special friend.

(*Speaking*) What am I going to call you, baby Dragon? What's your name?

The Dragon shakes his head

But you *must* have a name. (*Seeing the audience*) Perhaps ... can anyone think of a good name for a baby Dragon?

He encourages the audience to shout out suggestions. Rupert and his friends gather them. Pong Ping suggests various names, till the Dragon chooses one. For example, "Ming"

Ming! He likes it! (*He sings*)

Song 9: Baby Dragon Baby

Whichever name has been chosen is obviously used throughout the song

> Ming
> You're our baby Dragon baby,
> Ming
> We love you and we don't mean maybe,
> Ming
> You're our baby Dragon baby,
> Ming
> We love you baby,
> Baby Dragon baby.

All   Baby Dragon,
> Baby Dragon baby,
> Baby Dragon,
> Baby Dragon baby ...

Pong Ping (*speaking*) Stop! Tell you what, why doesn't everybody join in the song, to show Ming how many friends he's got. (*To the audience*) Would you like to do that?

Audience Yes.
Pong Ping You would?
Audience Yes.
Pong Ping Great! Every time his name crops up in the song, I'll wave and
 you shout it out! Like this ... (*He conducts them*)
All Ming! Ming! Ming!

They sing

Audience	Ming
All	You're our baby Dragon baby,
Audience	Ming
All	We love you and we don't mean maybe.
Audience	Ming
All	You're our baby Dragon baby,
Audience	Ming
All	We love you baby,
	Baby Dragon baby.
	Baby Dragon
	Baby Dragon baby
	Baby Dragon
	Baby Dragon baby

Pong Ping   Who's the bravest Dragon that you've ever met?
All (including Audience) Ming
All   The baby Dragon.
Pong Ping   Who's the Dragon who is gonna be my pet?
All   Ming
All (including Audience) The baby Dragon.

Audience	Ming
All	You're our baby Dragon baby,
Audience	Ming
All	We love you and we don't mean maybe.
Audience	Ming
All	You're our baby Dragon baby,
Audience	Ming
All	We love you baby,
	Baby Dragon baby.

> Baby Dragon,
> Baby Dragon baby,
> Baby Dragon,
> Baby Dragon baby,
> Baby Dragon,
> Baby Dragon baby ...

All (including Audience) Ming!

Music continues as everyone starts to leave. Pong Ping takes the Dragon with him. All wave goodbye, thanking Edward for his party

SCENE 4

Nutwood Common

Rupert, alone, starts his journey home

He reaches Wise Owl's tree

Rupert (*calling*) Wise Owl!

Wise Owl appears from his hole in the tree

Wise Owl You've woken me up again, little bear.
Rupert Just to say thank you for your advice.
Wise Owl Did you take it? Did you visit the Clerk of the Weather?
Rupert Yes. And look!
Wise Owl You got your sunny day! (*Yawning*) Well done, Rupert. Well done!

Rupert goes on to Squirrel's tree

Squirrel appears

Rupert Hallo, Squirrel, how are you?
Squirrel Fine, Rupert. Spring is here.
Rupert I know.
Squirrel It's warm enough for my babies to leave the nest. (*Calling*) Come along, babies. They loved your peanut butter sandwich, Rupert. Thank you.

The baby squirrels, squeaking noisily, appear on the branch

Rupert Bye, Squirrel! Bye baby squirrels!

He does a circuit of the stage as the scene changes to:

SCENE 5

Rupert's Home — exterior

Mr Bear is looking at his window box and/or hanging basket. There is washing on the line

Rupert arrives. Music plays through the scene

Rupert Hi, Dad!
Mr Bear Hallo, son. Good day?
Rupert Fine, Dad.
Mr Bear Fine for me too, son. The weather's bucked up at last. Look!

He shows Rupert his window box and/or hanging basket — suddenly flowers visibly grow from them

   Mrs Bear comes out of the door with a washing basket

Mrs Bear Hallo, Rupert.
Rupert Hi, Mum.
Mrs Bear What a lovely sunny day! (*She goes to the washing line*) And my
   washing's beautifully dry! (*She starts unpegging it and putting it in the
   basket*)
Rupert Good.
Mrs Bear Tea's on the table and then it's bedtime.
Rupert Thank you, Mum.

Rupert goes inside

Mr Bear Springtime in Nutwood. The best time of the year!

The Lights fade as the scene changes to:

SCENE 6

Rupert's Bedroom

Rupert is in bed, reading a book

Mr and Mrs Bear enter

Mrs Bear How was Edward's party?
Rupert Good, Mum, really good.
Mr Bear And what did you give him for a present, son?
Rupert A sunny day.
Mr Bear Oh, Rupert ...
Rupert I did, Dad. I went to the Clerk of the Weather, up in the sky beyond the clouds. He fixed it!
Mrs Bear (*smiling*) Listen to him, Dad. He's still in Cloud Cuckoo Land!
Rupert I went there too, Mum. Saw the Cuckoos! Then there was the Green Dragon. And Zita.
Mr Bear Oh Rupert, you live in a dream world!
Mrs Bear But we love you. Night, Rupert.
Rupert Night, Mum. Night, Dad.
Mr Bear Night, Rupert.

They go, turning off the light. But Rupert is still visible

Rupert (*to the audience*) It wasn't a dream, was it? I really did see the Clerk of the Weather, didn't I?

He suddenly remembers something — from under the sheets he brings the miniature barometer the Clerk of the Weather gave him. He smiles. He holds on to it. He goes to sleep

Fade to Black-out

> *Lights up for the Curtain Call, which is in fact the end of the Nutwood School Concert. The "Nutwood School Concert" banner is back. Ottoline at the piano returns. If necessary, Rupert's bedroom could remain on stage, upstage of the action*

Rupert gets out of bed and steps forward to sing

Song 9A: Goodbye From Nutwood

(*Singing*)   N.U.T.
Double U Double O D
Nutwood! Nutwood!
That's the place to be;
Nutwood is the place for me!

The others enter

Ottoline   And me!
Algy   And me!
Podgy   And me!
Bill   And me!
Edward   And me!
Mr Bear   And me!
Mrs Bear   And me!
Pong Ping And me!

The Green Dragon enters

All   And him!

N.U.T.
Double U Double O D
Nutwood! Nutwood!
That's the place to be;
Nutwood is the place for me!

So dim the lights,
Time to go,
Stop the music,
It's the end of the show.

We've said our words
And sung each song,
Happy that
You came along.

Rupert   We hope that you are
Glad you came.

                    Don't forget us
                    Or the name
                    Of

All   N.U.T.
                    Double U Double O D
                    Nutwood! Nutwood!
                    That's the place to be
                    Nutwood is the place for me!

                    Nutwood! Nutwood!
                    Now our concert ends
                    Time to say goodbye from —

The following lines are spoken

Ottoline   Ottoline!
Algy   Algy Pug!
Podgy   Podgy Pig!
Bill   Bill Badger!
Edward   Edward Trunk!
Mrs Bear   Mrs Bear!
Mr Bear   Mr Bear!
Pong Ping   Pong Ping!
All   The Green Dragon!
Rupert (*singing*) Rupert and friends!

All (*singing*)   Rupert and friends!
                    Rupert and friends!

Black-out

Reprises as required

CURTAIN

FURNITURE AND PROPERTY LIST

Only essential furniture and properties are listed here. Further dressing may be added at the director's discretion.

ACT I
SCENE 1

On stage: Piano
Banner: "Nutwood School Concert"
Dumbbells

Off stage: Handbell, notes (**Dr Chimp**)
Thick rope (**Edward Trunk**)
Oriental spinning plates with sticks (**Pong Ping**)
Cardboard box (**Algy Pug**)
3 apples (**Bill Badger**)
"Doll's House" containing soft-toy Rupert (**Tigerlily, Chinese Conjuror**)
Envelopes (**Edward Trunk**)

Personal: **Algy Pug**: giant rubber joke fly, tap on a string, kettle
Chinese Conjuror: wand
Rupert: school satchel containing peanut butter sandwich

SCENE 2

Personal: **Rupert**: hanky

SCENE 3

On stage: Broom
Watering can
Frozen washing, including one very stiff shirt (on washing line)

Off stage: Washing basket

SCENE 4

Strike: Broom
Watering can
Washing basket

On stage: Book

SCENE 5

Strike: Book

Off stage: Kite (**Pong Ping**)
                 Music case (**Ottoline**)
                 Pram containing Baby Badger puppet (**Bill Badger**)
                 Bag containing buns (**Podgy Pig**)
                 Boxes of food, party hats, etc. for party (**Edward Trunk**)
                 Bicycle or pogo stick (**Algy Pug**)

SCENE 6

On stage: Oriental sideboard. *On it:* three glasses, opaque "Lotus vase"
                 Tin with jack-in-the-box snake

Off stage: Magic wand (**Tigerlily**)
                 Oriental magic cabinet (**Tigerlily** and **Pong Ping**)

SCENE 7

Strike: Oriental sideboard
                 Oriental magic cabinet

ACT II
SCENE 1

No props required

SCENE 2

On stage: Instruction manual

Personal: **Clerk of the Weather**: miniature barometer

SCENE 3

Off stage: Birthday presents (one of them a toy trumpet) and long banner: "Happy
                 Birthday to Edward Trunk" (**Pong Ping**, **Bill Badger**, **Tigerlily**,
                 Algy Pug and **Podgy Pig**)
                 Birthday cake with lighted candles (**Bill Badger**)

SCENE 4

No props required

SCENE 5

On stage: Washing (unfrozen) on washing line

Off stage: Washing basket (**Mrs Bear**)

SCENE 6

On stage: Book

LIGHTING PLOT

Various interior and exterior scenes
Practical fittings required: flashing lights, display screen etc. for console, Act II, Scene 2

To open: Fade House Lights as bell is rung; bring up full stage lighting

ACT I, SCENE 1

Cue 1	**Rupert**: " ... crossing Nutwood Common." *Crossfade to* SCENE 2	(Page 9)

ACT I, SCENE 2

Cue 2	**Rupert** circles the stage for the scene change *Crossfade to* SCENE 3	(Page 11)

ACT I, SCENE 3

Cue 3	The music continues after the song has finished *Fade lighting and crossfade to* SCENE 4	(Page 13)

ACT I, SCENE 4

Cue 4	**Mr** and **Mrs Bear** turn off the light *Black-out*	(Page 16)

ACT I, SCENE 5

Cue 5	When ready *Bring up dawn effect; fade up lighting throughout scene*	(Page 16)
Cue 6	Thunder *Darken for thunderstorm/snowfall*	(Page 21)
Cue 7	The **Snowbird** enters *Bring up lighting on* **Snowbird** *against the blacks*	(Page 22)
Cue 8	The **Snowbird** calls farewell and exits *Crossfade to* SCENE 6	(Page 23)

ACT I, Scene 6

ACT I, Scene 7

ACT II, Scene 1

To open: Suitable lighting for UV/puppetry sequence

ACT II, Scene 2

ACT II, Scene 3

Cue 21   All wave goodbye to **Edward**   (Page 56)
             Crossfade to SCENE 4

ACT II, SCENE 4

Cue 22   **Rupert** does a circuit of the stage for scene change   (Page 57)
             Crossfade to SCENE 5

ACT II, Scene 5

Cue 23   **Mr Bear**: " ... best time of the year!"   (Page 57)
             Crossfade to SCENE 6

ACT II, Scene 6

Cue 24   **Mr and Mrs Bear** turn off the light   (Page 58)
             Reduce to dim light

Cue 25   **Rupert** goes to sleep   (Page 58)
             Fade to black-out

Cue 26   When ready   (Page 58)
             Lights up for curtain call

Cue 27   When song finishes   (Page 60)
             Black-out; reprises as required

EFFECTS PLOT

ACT I

Cue 1	**Audience** (*conducted by* **Tigerlily**): "Abracadabra!" *Flash*	(Page 5)
Cue 2	" ... crossing Nutwood Common." *Background birdsong; continue throughout Scene 2*	(Page 9)
Cue 3	**Squirrel**: "Atishoo!" *High-pitched chattering from tree*	(Page 10)
Cue 4	**Squirrel**: "Atishoo!" *More chattering*	(Page 10)
Cue 5	To open SCENE 5 *Birdsong throughout scene*	(Page 16)
Cue 6	**Baby Badger** pops his head out of the pram *Screaming and crying from baby*	(Page 17)
Cue 7	**Pong Ping**: "Sorry." *Baby screams*	(Page 18)
Cue 8	**Bill Badger**: "He's my friend." *Baby screams*	(Page 18)
Cue 9	**Pong Ping**: "Edward Trunk's just —— " *Crash, off*	(Page 19)
Cue 10	**Rupert** and **Pong Ping** set off, to music *Crack of thunder*	(Page 21)
Cue 11	**Rupert**: "Quick!" *Snow starts to fall; it becomes more blizzard-like*	(Page 21)
Cue 12	**Tigerlily** waves the wand *Flash*	(Page 26)
Cue 13	**Tigerlily** waves the wand *Flash*	(Page 26)

Cue 14   **Audience**: "Rupert, ready, steady, go!"   (Page 28)
              Flash

Cue 15   **All**: " ... two, one, lift off!"   (Page 31)
              Sound effects for take off; dry ice effect

ACT II

Cue 16   **Clerk**: "Yes ..."   (Page 38)
              Dials and cogs on console start working

Cue 17   **Clerk of the Weather** activates the screen   (Page 39)
              Slides, video or computer graphics on screen during song

Cue 18   **Rupert**: "I will. Thank you."   (Page 41)
              The screen goes fuzzy

Cue 19   **Clerk**: "What on earth ... ?"   (Page 41)
              Zita's *face appears on the screen*

Cue 20   As **Zita** enters the Weather Station   (Page 42)
              Flash; the picture on the screen suddenly disappears

Cue 21   **Rupert** and the **Dragon** start to fly off   (Page 47)
              Whooshing sound effect

Cue 22   **All** cheer   (Page 52)
              A clock chimes three times

Cue 23   Flowers grow   (Page 53)
              Birdsong